FLOW

Procrastination and ADHD Cure for Productivity Subconscious Morning Re-Programming Hypnosis-like NLP Script

By
Daniel Ben Abraham

Daniel Ben Abraham Publishing, LLC
USA

1

DANIEL BEN ABRAHAM

ISBN: 979-8-9878410-1-3

First published in the United States of America

Morning Programming

Introduction and disclaimer

This content is like operating programming for your mind. Keep this book by your bed and look at it first thing in the morning, even before your phone, because your phone gives you a dopamine kick. Reach for this book as soon as you wake up.

This is not a video nor an app, because you need to gently push your own thoughts through your own mind in your own voice. Reading this script every day helps accomplish that. Why not motivational videos? Videos spike your dopamine while viewing them, but then your dopamine drops throughout the day. These books are designed to use your subconscious to correct actions and behavior patterns when you're *not artificially* spiking, or when other urges might hit. I started writing these for myself for this purpose.

This book contains general content designed to help you reshape behavior and thought patterns to improve your habits and lifestyle. These reprogramming books contain suggestions designed to help your mind process your thoughts differently and form habits to help you achieve greater success, wealth, health, abundance, and other benefits with more positive mental attitudes. It is intended for people who need to incorporate more positive and constructive suggestions into their thought processes. If any of the content does not suit your goals, adjust them. Do not use any content you feel does not serve your goals. None of this is medical advice, psychological advice, financial advice, health advice, or any other professional advice. Apply the content in this book with the advice of professionals, as this book contains general guidelines only. You must consult your all appropriate and licensed professionals, doctors, nutritionists, psychologists, psychiatrists, business advisors, lawyers, accountants, financial advisors, and other professionals to know what is right for you, and use accordingly. If any of the content does not suit your goals, adjust them. Use of this book is at your discretion and entirely your own risk. By using this book, you agree to hold the author and all agents thereof harmless of any results, foreseeable or unforeseeable.

This book is simple, quick, and easy to read. The point is that you read it again and again. You don't read it for the information. You read it so your brain can go through the exercises of processing these messages. It's simple. It's written with a pleasant tone, and

Morning Programming

almost entirely positive language to allow your brain to absorb and build pathways around this content. Don't just read these. Try to internalize as you read these messages for at least 5 minutes every day, feel the meaning associated with these messages to your life. In your mind, see yourself doing things correctly in your day to day. Feel the positive results you want coming true, and feel the positive emotions and associations with your life and accomplishing your goals. Choose your favorite messages and repeat them to yourself in your mind as your mantra throughout the day. Internalize it. You are reprogramming your mind through repetition and positive emotion. You can open this book and start reading anywhere, and read as much as feels good for you. Try to think of the positive messages throughout the day until the thoughts and connected actions become habit. Try it for 30 days consistently.

You may notice interesting or colorful language, run-on sentences, repetition, disorganization, plays on words, poetic, rhyme, and rhythmical and other unusual word and sentence structures and even grammatical and logical errors and inconsistencies. These are all intentional, and part of the re-

Morning Programming

programming process, as is reading this daily. Just relax and go with it.

When this works for you, tell your friends, give me a review on Amazon, and link to me. Check out more books from this series for improving other areas of your life.

Follow me for more:
Tw: @thepeacematrix
Tw: @danielbabraham1
www.danielbenabraham.com

Good Morning!

Today is an opportunity.

When I wake up in the morning, the first thing I do is look at this document. I made the decision to do this, and sticking with my decisions feels good.

I am on a self-improvement journey that I love, and love myself for doing.

Self-improvement gives me meaning and happiness. That's why when I wake up in the morning, the first thing I do is look at this document.

I am improving by taking positive steps and avoiding negative steps on this journey.

As I read this, I feel gratitude – gratitude that I am moving my life in a good direction. It is empowering, and beautiful.

Taking on this challenge makes my life more beautiful because it is a journey of growth and achievement. Life is about me and my potential I'm exploring.

Morning Programming

I am venturing into a productive world where my mind works perfectly to help me accomplish my goals.

I know my goals must be accomplished step by step, and this effort is about taking each little step in the journey towards my goals.

I realize that nobody can achieve respectable goals doing only what they feel like when they feel like.

I have made the decision to improve myself, and I am, because that is who I am.

I am super productive.

I am hyper-productive.

I am ultra-productive.

I am mega-productive.

I move quickly and easily from one correct thought to the next. I flow quickly and easily from one correct task to the next.

And my magic word for my new lifestyle is FLOW.

Morning Programming

I know my next task. I know it clearly. I know it exactly. I know it in my core. I know it inside and out.

I can see my next task in my mind.

I keep my next task in the forefront of my mind.

I can see myself taking the next action in my mind.

I can see the exact, precise next action.

And I take action.

And I see my next action.

And I organize my thoughts and actions and take the next one.

And I build from there.

I act.

I act so I will not wonder what would have happened had I acted sooner.

Morning Programming

I act.

I act on my thoughts.

I act on action.

The universe likes action.

The universe likes momentum.

In one moment, I gain momentum.

I go from physical action to mental action.

I go from mental action to physical action.

I go from one constructive thought to the next.

I go from one constructive action to the next.

I am in flow.

I plan my days and tasks. I write out every detail.

I am constantly aware of my plans for best use of my time.

Morning Programming

I breathe in.

I breathe out.

I am calm and relaxed.

Planning what I will do is time well spent, and pays dividends in return in increased productivity, which I love.

I replan my day throughout the day as needed.

I develop a routine for my morning tasks to be an effective and efficient launch to the start of every new day, and I perfect that routine.

I know that while being productive, I can still focus on the big picture. I know what my big goals are, and I know what actions they translate into every minute, hour, day, week, month, and year.

I know clearly my primary goal for the day.

I see it precisely.

Morning Programming

I see myself doing it mentally.

I put in the effort to see myself accomplishing it in my imagination clearly, and then actually doing it is so easy.

I always know exactly what I'm supposed to be doing, and thinking about, and I do good.

I move quickly and easily from one task to the next.

I remind myself throughout the day that "I move quickly and easily from one task to the next"

I breathe in, and out, calmly and happily.

I love moving towards my wonderful goals with each action I take, and I feel joy all day as I do.

It feels amazing to put effort into every thought and action, and know I am propelling my life forward.

I visualize myself going from one task to the next.

I see myself in my mind's eye working on my task until it is complete.

Morning Programming

I love the personal power I feel from controlling and disciplining my own mind and body. It gets easier with every effort.

I am a person of action.

My actions flow like a river in the direction of my goals.

I know that success is as much about not doing the not right things as it is about doing the right things. If I am not using my time most wisely on social media or the internet or games or whatever, I quickly catch myself and quit unproductive activities. For social media, I realize that the scrolling gesture of moving my finger or thumb upward is what keeps me and my brain attached, and I become very conscious of it. I quickly catch myself, close unproductive technologies, and get productive again quickly. I notice my opportunity to get free and escape, and I seize opportunity yes I do.

I have protection mechanisms in place in my mind to avoid the things I know I should avoid.

Morning Programming

When I fall into less than productive states, I quickly catch myself, and bring my mind to the best thoughts and actions.

Every morning I make a quick mental note of the specific things I want to avoid as unproductive, and I avoid those things.

I see my day unfold without unproductive things, and my day unfolds how I envision it, and my day is better and I feel pride.

I know that having the correct thoughts in my mind leads to my correct actions, and I love putting in the effort and pushing my thoughts back on track every time they get off.

I love the feeling of putting my focus into a task that moves me toward my goals.

I jump at every opportunity to push myself forward, and enjoy the task for its own sake.

I love becoming a perfectionist at tasks.

I love getting into a task and its details.

14

Morning Programming

I love the constant and steady flow of pleasure and joy that comes from being productive, effective, efficient, and focused... second by second, minute by minute, neuron by neuron.

My effort is its own reward.

I move quickly and easily from one constructive thought to the next, organized. I move quickly and easily from one task to the next.

I am thankful for my ability to focus.

Focusing feels satisfying.

I enjoy whatever I direct my focus on so I can do it well.

While my conscious mind is focused, my subconscious mind feels pleasure, joy, and gratitude that I am master of my own moment, and master of my own life.

I own my life. I'm buying it. I'm paying for it with my attention. It's mine now.

Morning Programming

I love reading this book. I love reading this book because I know that it brings me much closer to my goals quick.

I know that the faster I move through life taking action, the more I can accomplish in this lifetime, and the more satisfied I will be.

When I get unfocused, I catch myself, realize I am unfocused, and go right back to my task.

I catch myself instantly and immediately go back to my task, keeping my train of thought.

When I am to pull away from what I am focusing on, I immediately catch myself, and divert myself right back to my focus.

When I start to think of a different topic which is not what I should be thinking about, I immediately catch myself, take a breath, and refocus right back to what I should be thinking about.

I refocus on task easily and readily.

Morning Programming

Subconsciously, I'm ready for myself to get off track, and as soon as I do, I catch myself immediately, and breathe, and bring myself right back on track, and smile.

When I focus, I feel good in my heart and soul.

I know that I am moving closer to the life I want with every moment(um) of effort, and it feels amazing.

I realize being in flow state is not merely doing what I am supposed to be doing - it is thinking about what I am supposed to be thinking about.

Flowing through my mind are the thoughts that I should be thinking about at any given time in order to accomplish my goals for the minute hour, day, week, month, and year.

I use the power of thought to my advantage.

Focus is a super-power of mine, and with each effort, I learn how to control and wield it better and better to accomplish my goals.

I am focused like a laser, deep into my work.

Morning Programming

My thoughts are organized, clear, and effective.

I love meditating to clear my mind and make my mind work more effectively and efficiently.

I am always thinking about what I should be thinking about.

I always know the next action to take towards my goals.

I can decide what my next task is, see it clearly, figure it out, and take action.

I easily take the next incremental step, even if just looking at a document, or getting in front of my computer, opening something, finding an email, picking up the phone, looking at what I should be looking at, making a mental note of my next item on my To Do list, or getting myself into a position to do or learn or decide the next step.

I know about the law of incremental gains, and I love taking any small action towards my goals.

Morning Programming

I constantly see myself doing my next task in my mind, and then move and take physical action towards it.

When I have a thought of something I must do, I count backwards 5-4-3-2-1 and then I feel compelled and I move my body to action immediately with a burst of energy.

I see my next task, and move. I see, and move… like the moving sea, of what I need to do, to be who I want to be.

The greatest joy of life is to be who I want to be.

I breathe in, and I breathe out, calmly and productively.

When I think of a task that needs to be done, I easily move towards it and take the first step. If I don't know the first step, I envision figuring it out and move towards it. I move towards my goals. I gravitate towards them.

When I'm doing something and am pulled away, I immediately catch myself consciously and bring

Morning Programming

myself back to focus on task. I do this repeatedly and easily.

It feels great to push myself and decide to give myself more time in focus, and it happens more and more naturally.

I breathe in.

I breathe out.

My mind easily moves from one consecutive thought to the next, like going from 1 to 2 to 3 to 4 to 5.

I am super productive.

I am mega productive.

I am ultra productive.

I am in flow, as my mind moves from one correct thought to the next, and one correct action to the next.

I am in flow.

Morning Programming

My mind moves from one correct thought and action to the next.

Procrastination is anything other than doing my primary, clear goal.

When I catch myself, it's like an itch to jump to resolve by taking action.

Procrastination is a challenge I look forward to overcoming as soon as I catch myself.

When I catch myself procrastinating I work through the four reasons why, and get on task toward my goal.

I know the four reasons I procrastinate are 1. Fear, 2. decision needed, 3. Information or knowledge needed, and 4. Brain chemistry. Whenever I catch myself procrastinating, I work through these four reasons why, and get back onward toward my goal.

First, when I am afraid of something, I think of the reasons I may be afraid, I work through it, and get back to my goal. I know that to do something, I must make sure my fear is overpowered by my desire to do it.

Morning Programming

It feels amazing to be able to logically work through and conquer my fears.

I know my courage brings me further in life.

Second, when I have a decision to make, I make most decisions quickly and easily.

I get the information I need, and make a decision, and move on.

I love overcoming my fear and indecisiveness.

I love overpowering fear and indecisiveness every time I face it, and overcome it, and I feel joy, as I take each step beyond a challenge.

Decision-making is a muscle I am strengthening with each decision I make.

Even though I know some of my decisions will not be perfect, I know that making more decisions with more determination and sticking with them will get me farther in life.

Morning Programming

I am a decision-making machine.

I make firm and clear decisions and stick to them for the benefit of overall clarity and progress in my life.

I stick with my decision until I revisit the issue and make another clear decision.

Being a decision-maker and sticking with my decisions feels courageous, and I love pursuing life.

Third, when I don't know how to do something, I imagine how I might learn or figure it out, and then I jump on the opportunity.

I know that to do something, my lack of knowledge of the details, especially of the next step, must be filled!

I am hungry for the information I need to move past the next obstacle, and feel the joy of accomplishment.

I focus on the challenge with enthusiasm to figure it out and overcome it.

Morning Programming

When I don't know enough to know what to do next, I get the information I need, especially about the next step, I make a decision, I conquer my fears, and I act.

I am a person of action.

As it says in scripture, I tell myself I "go from strength to strength."

Fourth, when I don't have enough brain chemistry to start and stay on task, I use my mind to envision myself doing the next step, and I force that thought until it turns to my action.

I use my imagination to see myself doing right, and then I do right.

I think of and envision every detail of me doing the next step at the forefront of my mind with all my focus until it turns to action now.

I see myself clearly doing the next task and I do.

Thought → action

Morning Programming

I am amazingly focused, effective, efficient, and productive.

I think and move like a well-oiled machine.

I am in FLOW.

I think like a supercomputer, and I propel myself towards my next goal like an effective machine.

My thoughts and actions are organized perfectly, calmly, smoothly, flowing from one to the next.

I move quickly and easily from one task to the next.

My mind is a super effective machine.

My mind is a machine that can do everything I need to do to be incredibly, powerfully, productive.

I breathe in.

I breathe out.

I remember I am in flow throughout the day.

Morning Programming

I am calm and happy as I move toward my goals, optimistic.

I realized that for self-improvement, it doesn't matter how many times I get off track, and that I definitely will get off track. What matters is how quickly I realize I am on off-track and get back on.

When I noticed myself thinking about unproductive things, I gently guide myself back on track. Off course, on track. Of course, I am on track.

My life is on track and it feels wonderful. It's literally pleasurable to know that.

It's a pleasure to be me.

I love being in flow with the universe towards the real me.

I am in FLOW.

I love being in FLOW.

My views are pro-duck-tivity, and I am for this viewpoint, and in favor of this flavor of productivity.

Morning Programming

Productivity feels good. My mind and heart are soothed in pleasure from productivity all day long.

Each challenge is an opportunity to see a task, do it, move ahead, and grow.

The more I push my brain to function, and function better, the better it functions for me.

My brain is like a pencil that I am sharpening with my efforts. My mind works like a smooth-running engine.

My brain is my friend.

Anything I make a note of, I remember right when I need to. My memory is improving with every little effort I love putting into my mind.

I am my own best self-improvement project, and it is a joy of my life.

I realize that in order to change what I do, I have to change who I am, and I constantly use my mind to shape the individual that I am with each thought and action.

Morning Programming

I am organized, productive, effective, strong, disciplined, and powerful, and being my true self makes me happy.

I am happy to know that I am taking best advantage of every blessed moment given to me.

I always know exactly what is next on my "To Do" list, and that's what I spend my time thinking about and doing. It's at the forefront of my mind.

My heart will cry tears of joy that I am productive.

I love being so productive that I am in flow.

I love being in a flow state of amazing efficiency and effectiveness because it feels good. Simply and honestly, it feels good. What a feeling of accomplishment and satisfaction.

It feels pleasurable in the brain and the body, and my mood is happier and joyous, because I am moving myself forward in life with my own energy.

I am calm, energized, and happy.

Morning Programming

I am strong, effective, and efficient.

I am more efficient than a fish who finished their task.

I bask in my task.

Flow is when my brain works effectively and efficiently, and my brain works effectively and efficiently, gets into flow easily, and loves being in flow.

If I fall out of flow, I get right back into flow.

I love being in FLOW.

I love reading this book. It feels good to read this every morning and it pays dividends in my effectiveness.

I am organized, focused, and move quickly and easily from one task to the next. It is the path to a better life.

Morning Programming

Thinking of the things that I want, I know that by being in flow I am bringing these things closer to my reality.

What would my life be like without flow? What is my life like with beautiflow flow?

I move like raindrops.

My actions flow toward my goals like a river.

Flow is a way of thinking. Flow is a state of mind. Of positive brain chemicals flowing so I can be my best.

Flow is a way of putting more effort and energy into my thought organization so that my brain does more of what I know it should, automatically.

Throughout the day, I think of being in flow. I crave flow. I think of the beauty of flow. I love flow. I think of my pure joy that comes out of being in flow. And I go to my task and get in flow.

Positive energy is flowing through me all the time.

Morning Programming

As my constructive thoughts flow from one to the next.

As my movements flow.

And my actions flow to success after success.

I know that when I dive deep into something and get really into it, I can do amazing things in that, so one of my goals is to find a hobby or career in an area I love going so deep into.

I realize many tasks need to get done. Flow is about doing all of these things. Some people find flow through music. Some people find flow through meditation. I find myself in flow.

I think of my big, long-term goals.

I think of the most important things that I want for my life to be fulfilled; to be happy and satisfied and secure, and joyous throughout my day.

I want to have meaning and delicious challenges that make life just the right amount of exciting.

Morning Programming

Once I know my major long-term goals, then I see my smaller goals and know them.

I love thinking about my goals, big and small.

Each day as I read this, I pause and reflect for a moment and think about my major life and long-term goals, and my medium-term goals, and my short term goals.

I pause and imagine my goals.

I dive into my goals like a delicious pool.

I bathe in my goals because they are wonderful.

My goals are amazing parts of my life path.

I know desire is the source of all achievement, and I am hungry.

My goals are the path to amazing new wonderful character-building experience.

I am growing and deepening as I pursue my goals.

Morning Programming

My goals are some of the most beautiful things in life.

My adventure warms my heart.

When I think of myself, I like myself.

I like myself with a warm, fuzzy, feeling because I am on my own adventure.

I love building my best life. I love every little task in the process of building my best life.

When I know my long and medium-term goals, I think of my short-term goals. I see clearly what I am aiming at.

My little tasks bring me closer.

I grow from pursuing my goals, and the more and better I aim, the better I hit my targets.

My brain develops through my willpower of pushing myself, as I take one breath and one action towards my goals. It feels amazing.

Morning Programming

I know that if I improve just a little bit, every day and consistently, I will really see my goals real through my delightful efforts.

Pursuit of my goals is my new fun for me.

It's a beautiful adventure to look in the mirror and know that I fought hard today; I pushed myself just a little more. I look at myself in the mirror with a satisfied smile, and I embrace that challenge that I am going through every day to become a new, slightly better me.

I chisel myself out of stone.

I keep my major life goals and big goals and medium goals in the back of my mind.

I remind myself of my goals at least once a day, and my goals are the first things I think of when I wake up in the morning and they just feel good all over.

I think of my short-term goals and tasks, and keep them in forefront of my mind.

Morning Programming

I think of what I have laid out in my To Do list, and think about how each little thing that I do improves my life by one small degree, and brings me closer to those big, beautiful goals.

I am blessed to have this moment, and I use it to build fractional improvements in my life, one on top of the next, like one foot in front of the other, one moment to the next, one thought to the next.

Each little wonderful and delightfully-satisfying bit of effort that I put in makes a difference, and it gives me joy. And because it gives me joy, I am able to do these things easier and easier.

I move quickly and easily from one task to the next.

I am in flow throughout my day as I work deeply on my goals.

I know who I am though my efforts.

My mind is conscious and present on what I should be doing. If I stray, I come right back. If I drift off, I catch myself and come right back to what I'm supposed to be doing.

Morning Programming

It is easy to take a small bit of action to get back on track.

If I'm not on track and on my phone, I quickly and easily catch myself, feel the strength to put down my phone, and get back on track.

I refocus as often as I need to, and it feels good every time to be strong and in control.

I repeat in my mind my mantra throughout the day, as I move: "I move quickly and easily from one task to the next."

I move quickly and easily from one task to the next.

I am in FLOW.

I am in love with my controlling body that I am in love with controlling under my control.

Self-control is self-love.

Morning Programming

I am consciously aware of when my attention is not on what I am supposed to be focused on, and I easily bring myself to focus where I can be my best self.

When I get off course, I instantly correct. Off course, I correct. Of course I am correct in correcting myself when I am off course. My actions are correct.

I love flowing into flow, being in flow, as my thoughts smoothly flow from one productive thought to the next.

I love you, me!

I love that my brain chemicals are flowing, smoothly, peacefully, calmingly.

I breath to relax and stay on track.

I'm in flow. That's my zone. It's my play.

Being into my task is my playtime. It feels so good to be really deep into it.

Morning Programming

I love the pleasure from being focused on the details of my task, going from one thought smoothly to the next.

I breathe in, and out calmly.

I love the constant flow of pleasure, second by second, minute by minute, of making progress in a task.

I feel satisfaction from focus alone.

While my conscious mind is focused, my subconscious mind feels pleasure, it feels joy and gratitude that I am master of my own moment and master of my own life.

I own this moment that I am now the master of myself in.

I get a feeling of accomplishment from being in flow throughout the day. I can think while I'm moving, and I move quickly and easily from one task to the next.

I am accountable to myself and I move productively from task to task like one two three four.

Morning Programming

These values and ideas are implanted in my mind. They go deep down to my core. I notice myself doing them automatically.

I notice myself adding a little bit more effort, and making all the difference.

When I need to do something, I jump at it and start.

I know once I start doing something, it's much easier to continue doing it.

I just start.

I tell myself to do just 10 seconds…

It's easier to start something with just a little bit of effort I now love putting in.

And I'm constantly reminded with one word, flow.

I put in the effort and my life flows to prosperity.

It's like a force of nature. I am nature in motion.

Morning Programming

My mind enjoys being on the present task, my eyes focus on it, my attention gravitates to it.

My brain chemistry makes my work fun and enjoyable and interesting no matter what it is.

I get into whatever I'm supposed to be doing.

I do a qualityjob as the task and my goals require.

Sometimes, throughout the day, I pause, I take a deep breath, I relax, and I think of the most wonderful and relevant goal that I'd like to have. And I realize am in flow.

I realize that when I have something I'm supposed to be doing, I seek to know clearly what it is that I'm supposed to be doing, and I do it.

I love my task.

My task is my present little goal like a little mission that I have to accomplish today now instantly.

The best time to accomplish my task is right now.

Morning Programming

I enjoy the satisfaction of completing my task.

I enjoy the process of being in the mode of doing my task. I get into it.

The act of accomplishing slowly step-by-step with each word and each action of my hand with each thought in my mind of that activity feels good. It is all part of the productive completion.

Completion isn't just after I've finished and can sigh a deep breath of relief. Completion is every little act and step and thought in the process of that activity, and I love it all.

I love organizing my day and my life, I love planning my day, I love planning my week, I love planning my month. I love being organized inside my mind.

I love being organized in my schedule and planner.

These all feel amazing.

It is true freedom to be in control of myself. To be in control of my own mind.

Morning Programming

It is a delight to know that my mind spends its time doing what I should be doing.

I set aside time every day for everything that I need to do. Cutting out unproductive time, everything is possible.

I love meditating, and meditating helps me accomplish my goals.

I love exercise, and exercise helps me accomplish all my goals.

I delight in sticking to my health and personal habits based on my goals I set for myself.

I write out my goals and look at them every day. I am curious about their details.

My mind feels happy when I know my present goal. I always know my present goal and keep it in the forefront of my mind. If my thoughts wander and I think of something creative, I'll write it down and go back to my present goal.

Morning Programming

If I have wandered away from what I should be doing, I immediately realize it, and have a burst of amazing self-control, and immediately stop what I'm doing and go back to the task that I am supposed to be doing to accomplish my purposely-designated activity for the moment.

I know that living a life of consciousness and presence and purpose is satisfying.

I know that every little goal and every little effort towards every little goal brings me towards my small, medium, big, and life goals by my efficiency.

When I realize how my thinking is improving, I breathe in and breathe out, and I smile.

I realized that I am taking control of my own mind, and I do.

Still.

Always.

I breathe in flow.

Morning Programming

I breathe out.

I am taking control of my conscious mind and my subconscious mind, and they are working better and better together with every minute, with little bit of energy that I put into me.

I love putting energy in and getting more energy out. Every little micro bit of energy and effort that I put into being focused in mind and passion on what I'm supposed to be, comes back to me, many times over and joy and satisfaction, from my goals, my growing character, and meaning in life from pursuing them.

When I watch the movie of my life, it's not just about the ending. It's about the journey of the adventurer, and all the challenges and tasks great and small, that I complete one after the other on my adventure.

I am learning, changing, growing, improving, with my own efforts. This energy feels delightful. Every moment.

I am in flow.

I love being in FLOW.

Morning Programming

I move quickly and easily from one task to the next.
I say throughout the day that I move quickly and easily
from one task to the next.

My mind is conscious, present, and focused on what I
should be focused on.

I love subconsciously knowing that I am doing exactly
what I have directed myself to do.

And I really really love that I can actually enjoy any
activity.

I tell myself to enjoy, and I can get into it and be
focused on it and do better at it with just a micro little
bit of increasing effort every time.

Just a little more effort than last time. Just a little
more effort than last time.

Soon my mind operates like a supercomputer.
Organized. Focused.

My body functions like a well-oiled machine.
Disciplined. In control.

Morning Programming

I am productive like a machine.

I love self-disciplining myself.

Self-discipline is sexy.

I love knowing I say something in my mind, give myself a direction, and my body carries out my wishes.

I realize the more I tell myself to do something and follow up with action, the more connected my neurons become between my thoughts and my actions.

Each time I order myself to act and then act, action easier it gets. I am training my brain like a muscle. I love that my body responds to my commands.

I think, and I do.

I flow from flow to flow, smoothly as my positive brain chemicals flow, and my thoughts and actions flow, doing my best, with joy flowing through me.

Morning Programming

What are the greatest feelings in the world is satisfaction with myself. And that comes from action, which comes from effort. Real effort is physical action. It is like an energy force that I can spark and channel and guide and control towards the action I'm doing.

I have the mental focus and am putting one thought after the other after the next.

I am logical, pragmatic, and helpful to accomplishing every moment, every second, every microsecond of my present goal.

I clearly focus on and envision my correct actions.

The next thing I know, I am instantly doing it, deep into it.
I move quickly and easily from one task to the next.

My productivity is growing by leaps and bounds. When people talk to me, I am present. I hear what they are telling me.

I listen to them and I appreciate every human connection. These people warm my heart, and I warm

Morning Programming

theirs in return. Just one of the little nuggets of each wonderful day.

Just a tiny little bit of bliss, that I feel throughout my day. Progress. Productivity. Effort. Accomplishments. Success. Bliss. Bliss. Blissy. Bliss. They feel good.

Ah the joy and pleasure and bliss I get from doing the things I know I should be doing to improve my life.

Oh, for the love of the task at hand. I am grateful that I have a chance right now to improve my life, and I seize it. I am grateful for every chance to grasp life.

Every task is an opportunity, and every opportunity is a task.

Opportunities are like wonderful, beautiful, sparkling gems that appear before my eyes. I notice them instantly. I hone in and focus on them.

My thoughts and energy and willpower gravitates towards my opportunities, and I quickly seize the opportunities I sees.

Opportunities to act are play time for the kid in me.

Morning Programming

I love play.

When I am doing what I should be doing, I am deep into it.

I am in flow and I love flow.

My thoughts flow consistently and congruently.

My mental focus is sharp and keen and acute.

I can retrieve and have at hand all of the information and ideas whenever I need them and however I want them.

I am deep into what I am doing, and I love it. I love shaping what I am doing like an artist painting a mural, a sculptor molding a piece of clay, or a builder building a house, beautiful and perfect, one step leading to the next, one level leading to the next, one segment leading to the next, connecting to the next.

My work is well thought-out, organized, and impressive. My work impresses myself and others, and I love feeling satisfaction from a job well done.

Morning Programming

I improved my life in the past, present, and future.

I saved myself with self-discipline.

There once was a person who took control of their thoughts, their actions, and their life... Want to know their story?

Now comes the adventure. I love it. I breathe in and breathe out deeply and take on my day with joy and enthusiasm. Let's do this!

When I think of something I need to do, I move instantly toward it, more and more. Like I'm hungry for each step in my journey.

I am like a hungry lion ready to hunt for every opportunity for progress in my day, week, and life. I go chase after my goals, and through every challenge, I advance and move forward.

I do everything I can to make sure success is assured.

I. Live. Life.

Morning Programming

I am productive.

I am effective.

I am efficient.

I am strong.

I am in control.

I am focused.

I am in the driver's seat, finally.

I am in action.

I have momentum.

I am in flow.

Morning Programming